LACONIC LYRIC

Also by Jim Gronvold

Back River

Oak Bones

Star Thistle

Pith & Piffle

Word and Mortar

Cogs Turning

Sphere Spun

Churnings

Laconic Lyric
poems by Jim Gronvold

Oak Ink Press
2025

Copyright © 2025 Jim Gronvold
All rights reserved

ISBN: 978-1-7362973-4-6

Book and cover design by Jeremy Thornton
Cover photo by Jim Gronvold
Author photo by Kathy Flynn

To order additional copies
or to contact the author, write:

Oak Ink Press
oakinkpress@icloud.com
or visit
www.jimgronvold.com

Dedicated to tellers of Truth

CONTENTS

I

Same Boat   3
Specks   4
Alarm Trucks   5
Clock   6
Old Airports   7
Runway   8
Barn   10
Sears Tower   12
Zoo   14
77th   16
78th   17
79th   18
Solo   19
Writing   20
Curse   21
Block   22
Unique Pique   23
Clear-Eyed   24
One Meditation   25
Raking   26
Yet   27

II

Pelicans 31

Curlews 32

Wing Span 33

Air Traffic 34

Feathered 35

Owl Speak 36

Mockingbird 37

Feeder 38

Pompeii Mosaic 39

The Boathouse
At Laugharne 40

Bay Dawn 41

San Pablo Bay 42

Point Reyes 43

Vigil 44

Decay 45

Gossamer 46

Mid Autumn   47
Road Shadow   48
December Light   49
Winter Gray   50
Morning Fog   51
Mist   52
Balmy   53
Drop   54
Tap   55
Highway   56
Black Hole Pothole   57
Mirage   58

III

On Balance 61

Sand 62

Impulse 63

Pulse 64

Consciousness 65

Reach 66

Interwoven 67

Curious 68

Need To Know 69

Then Again 70

Gravity 71

Purpose 72

Duration 73

Expectation 74

Text 75

Possible 76

Luck 77

Insatiable 78

Perception 79

Cycles 80

Near And Dear 81

Hesitation 82

Flown 83

Crumble Mumble   84

Or   85

Bits And Pieces   86

Simplicity   87

Anyway   88

IV

Melding   91

People   92

Short   93

Hands Held   94

Leap   95

Magnetic   96

Familiar   97

Drum   98

Lovers   99

Context   100

Common   101

Boredom   102

Ask   103

Fine-Tuning   104

Measure   105

Appearance   106

Contrast   107

Visions   108
Blind Spots   109
Them   110
Dispute   111
Misled   112
Pretense   113
Politicos   114
Primal   115
Reprisal   116
Choice   117
Repair   118
Similarity   119
Sown   120
Ripples   121
Novelty   122
Comforts   123
Secondhand Store   124
Dare   125
Wings   126

Acknowledgements   129

…to find a kind
of quiet balance…

I

Same Boat

We're in the same boat
on a star blown sea.

Gathered or alone,
joined by the journey

into all weathers
of an ever unknown

dragging our anchors
through history

as we argue our course
on a skipping stone.

Specks

Tied as we are
to one star

in an infinity
of planets and suns

any observer
could clearly see

a sky full of reasons
for humility

while we strut and spin
our grand designs

under a vastness
we barely imagine.

Alarm Trucks

The weekly clockwork
of trash-trucks at dawn

wakes me with
a screech of breaks

and hydraulic arms
lifting garbage cans

dumping scraps and
clanking containers

into their echoing
deep steel-drums.

The waste of a week
whisked away

by grumbling giants
that sniff out their prey

leaving a wake of
wrappers and crumbs

digesting detritus
and shredded poems.

Clock

There's a kind of
musical magic

in the quick tick
and click of a tock

so basic to
a classic clock.

A simple metric
of reliable rhyme

and rhythm, to unlock
a lyric of time.

Old Airports

When travelers
wore suits, and
Sunday skirts

airports were
launchpads to
an open sky.

There were rooftop
observation decks

where children
leaned over railings
in the wind

watching airplanes
take off or land

and then ran around
as if they could fly.

Runway

One wrong turn
down a dark road

near O'Hare Airport
in our Dad's Chevy

and two teens—
me driving—

passed an open gate
to a straightaway

miles from the
nearest terminal light.

With windows open
we flew through the night

howling the wild
bliss of our kind.

Until a deep roar
rose up from behind

and a 707 passed
on our right

shaking the Chevy
in its wake

while the whole car
seemed to levitate

and I fought to hold
the steering wheel

until I could turn—
speed back to the gate—

and escape a thrill
turned all too real.

Barn

Cold rain on
a dark Swiss road.

We were two
dripping hitchhikers

dumped in a downpour,
near an old barn.

So we crept in
and slept on tables

til just before dawn
when a creaking door

woke me in fright
and I leapt to the floor

expecting the worst
from an angry farmer.

But the man who appeared
held a wooden tray.

Coffee and chocolate!
For two intruders!

A generous gift
for two trespassers

surprised by a smile
that said all he need say

to brighten the road
through another damp day.

Sears Tower

He probably thought
I was some kind of clown.

A grown man
standing on his head
as the elevator sped down.

"Hey mister,
what're you doing?"
said the upside-down face
by a shoeshine box.

But before I could
even answer,
I saw all the coins
from my pocket fall up

and thought it the price
of my gravity high,
as I watched the kid
chase them around.

When the doors opened
at the ground floor,
I expected him
to just take off.

But that kid,
who had to work
for small change,
had collected mine
to hand back to me

which I declined,
thanking him for
his honesty—
while wishing there
had been more.

Zoo

From a path
above the path
by the bears

I saw a boy—
or a small man—

move behind
groups and
families

as if he was
one of theirs.

He would stand
as near to them
as he could

and laugh when
they laughed

or point where
they pointed—

until they'd notice,
and move away

leaving him
looking so
disappointed

that I knew
he was not just
lost in the zoo.

So I went to see
what I could do.

But by the time
that I got there
he'd disappeared
in the drifting crowd
as the crush
of sightseers grew.

77th

Our sorrows and joys
nourish us.

Laughter lightens
the weight of worry.

Sadness can strengthen
our empathy

for those who face
what we have known

or problems that
could be worse

and that no one
should bear alone.

78th

Fortunate we
to come to be
born on this sphere
of soil and sea.

This spinning stage
of calm and rage
that whispers and rings
with vitality.

This home to
small and tall beings
that each, and all,
in their own way

rewrite the lines
of our ever evolving
comic-dramatic
mortality play.

79th

My birthday awoke
with garbage trucks.

Air breaks cracked
the silent night.

Cans clattered
and bottles broke

the moonlit morning
of soft shadows.

My day opened
with a lucky sky

calm and clear,
blue and bright

with sunlit moments
that would multiply

right to the edge
of twilight.

Solo

Spring stalks span
the path I walk

at my own pace
in the green grace

of fallen Sun
on field and thicket

in a day without time
where I slowly stalk

a simple rhyme
to sow in my pocket.

Writing

Sometimes, when
the old cogs click

observations can
inspire a lyric

that spins sounds
close to music.

Or, at the least,
words that might stick.

Curse

For a labor-of-love
worker in verse

whose hammered words
might not be heard

one has to think
it would be worse

not to nurse
this curious curse

for as long as
it can be stirred.

Block

Wondering, too long,
over one word,
I walked into
a whispering wood

where everything
growing and flowing
made complex questions
seem absurd.

It wasn't the riddle
of a title that mattered,
or how it might
be understood.

But, rather, the running
stream that I heard,
and the stunning song
of an unseen bird.

Unique Pique

Whether software
or someone else

uses the words
I write or speak

for a feeling that
I might have found—

or a problem
that I've unwound—

it would be foolish
of me to think

that I'd said the unsaid,
or something unique.

Clear-Eyed

How brighter the stars
and sparkling sea,
seen through sober clarity.

How lighter the step
and stronger the stride
without the burden
of pie-eyed pride.

One Meditation

A skilled labor
of silence

that slowly stills
the brain's chatter

long enough
to catch its breath

and calm the clatter
of needless nonsense

to find a kind
of quiet balance

seems a sublime
use of one's time.

Raking

Raking up
fallen leaves,
I imagine their
brief history.

I recall their
Spring-green glory,
and how they sang
a Summer breeze

or calmly cast
a speckled shade,
before their age
made them fall.

And now they
crumble into crumbs,
after sharing the air
we all borrow.

And I know that in time
all attachments let go,
but also that now
is not tomorrow.

Yet

Until gravity
takes me back

to the elements
of land and sea—

that still race
and rest in me

on this the
only planet

I will, or wish
to, ever be—

I ponder its
powerful grace

and wonder at
its beauty.

II

Pelicans

Pelicans pass
in single-file.

A silent line dance
of airborne jockeys

riding ripples
of ocean breeze

cruising currents
of surface air

tilting wide wings
as far as they dare

to slide over waves
about to break

and nearly scratch
the crushing curls

that crest and crash
in their steady wake.

Curlews

The only one there—
between sand and Sun—
to reflect on
the ocean, was me.

And, Curlews, of course,
that being the source
of Curlew energy.

And, doubtlessly,
countless creatures.
too many to ever see

who, never the less,
were my company
on that quiet walk
by the whispering sea.

Wing Span

Cormorants hang out
their wings to dry
after shaking
and waging their tails.

Sun warms the stretch
of the Dragonfly
before their next
meal passes by.

And I pull shirttails
out like sails
to catch a breath
of bending sky.

Air Traffic

Vultures cruise
contours of hill.

Hawks rise
on sunlight.

Nestlings flap
a practice drill.

Hummingbirds argue
in split-second flight

and Warblers trill,
just out of sight

while I direct traffic
from lawn-chair height.

Feathered

Some birds stay with us
wherever we fly.

Coast to coast
Red Tails cry

and familiar songs
twitter or boast:

the cackle of Crow
or sly Magpie,

the click of Swallow
and chirp of Sparrow.

Comforting sounds
from East to West

nest in memories
and feather our rest.

Owl Speak

What words do owls
repeat in their phrase?

That Morris-code chorus:
"Hoot-De-Hoot—Hoot Hoot"

Is it meant to raise
the hair on their prey

or announce themselves
in an amorous way?

And since it sounds
like all they will say

it makes me wonder
what few words I'd find

to tell the world
what's on my mind.

Mockingbird

You sing the sounds
of your territory

making them part
of your own story

and recite them
as courtship displays

that can also sound
like poetic praise

for the chirps and trills
you loudly rephrase

in piercing pleas
that persevere

with the vocal skill
of a balladeer.

But must you always
sing so near?

Feeder

The chippering
morning chatter

of small birds
at the tall feeder

crouches the
stalking cat

trapped behind
a screen door

tapping his tail
on his jail floor.

Thwap-thwap,
rat-a-tat-tat.

His wishful whimper
suppresses a roar.

Pompeii Mosaic

A tarnished jewel
of tiny tiles

set like scales
in profiles of fish.

The tangible trace
of a history

of bright art buried
by volcanic ash

but rescued from
time's crushing clutch

to grace the wall
of a gallery

as the legacy
of an artist's touch.

The Boathouse At Laugharne

His words still wade
the estuary

and wash the shells
of inky pearls

where stanzas swept
up in swirls

on singing wings
of imagery

that clouds recite
in the memory

of a singer of skies
and grinding tides

whose echoes still ring
down dripping hillsides.

Bay Dawn

This bay dawn splashes
marsh and meadow

as the shrinking
eastern shore shadow

goes sinking below
the growing glow

that slowly slides
down these hills.

Dawn announced
by sparrow and crow

as sunlight fills valleys
to its noonday crescendo.

San Pablo Bay

Across the wide bay
small curtains of rain

drape distant hills
with slanting veils—

sliding shades
of shifting gray—

while, silent, high winds
plow cloud into sky

and I stand in their
wake, warm and dry

as the breadth, and depth,
of air fills my breath.

Point Reyes

A rising, falling,
chop and roll

of hills that bubble
with Oak and Bay Leaf

where deer float
through dappled shade

and cattle graze
a tilting grade.

Where valleys wander
and tan sands wade

through rolling edges
of deep ocean

from where the Sun
slides towards tomorrow

behind a quivering
line of horizon.

Vigil

Calla Lilies don't
tuck in to sleep.

Their time is too short
to just shut down.

Even beneath
the cover of night

they stand to catch
any moonlight

that might fall from
the starry deep

and brighten
a soft-white crown—

for as long a vigil
as they can keep.

Decay

Would I like Lilies less
if they lasted forever?

I think the answer
would have to be yes.

Do I like Lilies more
because they decay?

I'd have to say
what I've said before:

"The graceful and good
don't last as long
as we wish they would."

But their moment
is all that matters,
or all that ever should.

Gossamer

Looking up
a cloudless hill

sunlit silken strands
of sheer light appear.

Shimmering lines
adhere to leaves

and weave weeds
into gossamer webs

that spread over
fences and chairs.

So many threads
cross and connect

this world of objects
small spiders collect.

Mid Autumn

Seduced by air
as thin as a promise

of Summer returning
out of the blue.

Enchanted by sunlight,
though winter is due.

A breeze so fair
it's gentle touch

caresses Autumn
and reminds me of you.

Road Shadow

Driving a tunnel
of roadside trees

sunlight blinking
through sinking leaves

dapples the road
with mottled ripples

of shade-shifting
waves that splash

as they crash
over the windshield

and disappear
in a dashing flash

of Summer dripping
and slipping away.

December Light

Trees eclipse the noon Sun
at its low winter height

scattering bright shafts
that slide downhill

and crawl across
the leaf-drift slope

in silent ticks
of turning light

that spin the season
as they spill

through shadows shifting
towards early night.

Winter Gray

Winter Suns crawl
until they fall.

Too often, behind
curtains of gray.

Pale Moons dance
through wispy veils

chasing starlight
and their own tails—

night after night
and day after day—

until the clouds
of winter fray.

Morning Fog

This cool, damp,
coastal dawn
will brighten beyond
its gray beginning

and shed the fog
that caresses
and blesses
ocean hills
that rise and fall

through shifting shades
of daylight spinning
out of the shimmer
of lurking stars
that setting Sun
will later recall.

Mist

Fog fades into
itself, through

lighter shades
of its own shadow.

And disappears
in daylight

leaving traces
of mist on the sky

that vanish slowly
as they flow

from billow,
back to a sigh.

Balmy

This middle of
a morning in May

the air is a fair
whisper of sea

with a taste of
rare delicacy

that wafts over me
on its balmy way

from coastal hills,
east to the bay.

Drop

Clouds on the run.
Rain moving on.

A lily lip diamond
caught a splash of sun

and held my attention
with the spectrum it spun

until tree shadows
pulled their curtain

and the sparkling
spell was undone.

Tap

Listening, in bed,
to distant thunder—

before slipping into
sheltered slumber—

the ticking tap
of dripping rain

is drowned out
by winds whipping

swirling waves
that beat my shell

as I drift off
on a cushioned swell

to float above the
storm I'm under.

Highway

Fishbowl windshields
pass, face to face.

Sardine strangers
blink at each other

forever plunging
from place to place.

We once swam
oceans and rivers

before we dared
to slither ashore

and crawled into
an upright race

that defied gravity,
then learned to fly

and now drives on
into outer space.

Black Hole Pothole

Heavenly headlights
of shattered glass
sparkle across
an asphalt sky
spilling past us
as we skid by
in slow motion
and out of gear
on the worn tread
of our rolling sphere.

Cloud-curbs splashed
by tide-puddled pools
of skylit seas
on our shining drop
in the starlit swirl
of galactic jewels
flung among galaxies
sliding non-stop
in their spin around
and down dark drains
wheeling to where
all roads disappear.

Mirage

That shimmering
vision at road's end—

the glimmering that
holds our gaze—

is just a glaze
of rays that bend

through distant,
simmering, haze.

A wishful vision
that doubts suspend

for the moment
that they amaze.

On Balance

To trace
the endless
depth of stars
or kick the dust
of sun-dried trails.

To feel a fair
breath of air
off the depth
of distant seas
and wonder at
the vast expanse
you touch in an
unseen breeze.

Or to take a step
on wet sand—
where tides tease
weathered land—
is to feel the way
eternity weighs
against the weight
of fleeting days.

Sand

We are the sand
that rolls with tides—

the tear-dust torn
by sun and storm.

We are the word
that time rides

and wings that
thoughts transform.

We are the flame
our breath provides

that when we share,
will keep us warm

and where the light
of hope abides

in its ever
evolving form.

Impulse

In the space
between spaces—
between shadows
of shadow—

at the center of being
where impulse flows
through the core of self
where awareness glows

webs of spark
too small to see
rush through streams
of senses and dreams

on shifting storms
of blood and sea
that dance and die
with the wild grace

of any fate
a life might face
on this pulsing plane
of possibility.

Pulse

The essence
of our presence

is a passing pulse
of impermanence.

The common core
of our mystery

is our energy
and awareness

of all we feel
and what we see—

the harshness
and the beauty.

Consciousness

If consciousness
could see itself

would it's reflection
fit in a mirror

or make its presence
any clearer?

Would it split prisms
of cosmic light

and open facets
of deep insight?

Or scream at the stars
in mortal fright?

Or laugh itself
to sleep at night

content with a sense
of self-awareness?

Reach

To care beyond
the life you know

for people where
you may never go

who say what you say
in a different way

but have feelings
much like your own

is, in a way,
to not be alone.

Interwoven

The weave of We
is interwoven

by flesh and bone,
dream and reason.

Threaded vines
of varied tone

bind us as they
rise and wind

from seed to bloom,
strung together

in patterns of
long spun design

on this star-lit loom
of ripples sliding

side to side, on
the wide unknown—

circle on circle
and line over line.

Curious

Why do we chase
the hint of a star

or need to search
some far shore?

Why not enjoy
where we are

and what we have
without wanting more?

These questions might
answer themselves

since, even to ask
is a way we explore.

Need To Know

The deep flow
of consciousness

at the heart
of understanding

and our innate
desire to survive

both drive our
need to know.

And though knowing
is never complete

we seek answers
that resonate

with the questions
we need to repeat.

Then Again

So many answers
we thought we knew

before we sought
a wider view.

Now in daylight,
or on review

they might not fit
the lines we drew

around the things
we thought were true

or all that we
set out to do.

But there are still
dreams to rescue

and other solutions
for us to pursue.

Gravity

Why does all rising
need to descend?

Why must this flight
of feelings end

and all of our
senses decompose

like fallen trees
returning to land

or all our words
drifting to echoes?

I suppose I should
try to understand

why laws of Nature
seem to demand

that everything
falls as it flows

and that is just
the way it goes.

Purpose

We may ask ourselves
why we're here.

But what if there's
no right answer?

What if it's all just
minute to minute

person to person,
year after year

and what matters most
is that we're still here?

Duration

In the grand scheme,
or stream, of things—

depending on
your point of view—

most of us, rather,
all but a few

are forgotten in
a generation or two.

Which should clarify
the real value

of all the best
we try to do

regardless of
its short duration.

Expectation

Expectations
exact their price

even before
the bills come due.

They spend our
savings against
advice

and rarely return
what they withdrew

or bet our future
on a roll of dice

as if but to wish
would make it true.

Text

Life itself—
honestly read—

is both history
and sacred text.

A journey through
cause and effect.

A tale told by
science and song

of weak and strong
points that connect

in real lessons
of right and wrong

with hints at what
might happen next.

Possible

Without wishful
thinking, would we
wither with worry
and just waste away?

Or would we then
be more inclined
to find some
peace of mind
in the possible
pleasures of
the present day?

Luck

Luck's not something
a wish can hold

or more than a name
for wild chance.

It's the shifting way
that things unfold

in this fluid churn
of circumstance

and unexpected
consequence.

An incident
of coincidence

the wishful
will romance.

Insatiable

The thirst no words
would quench.

The hunger no
feast could sate.

The answer no
reason will satisfy

is perfection no
wish should await.

Perception

The magic is in
the amazement.

The amazement
in the surprise.

Perfection is
a perception

of fiction
we fantasize.

The miracle is
in the moment

that we stop
to realize.

Cycles

Light and dark
circle each other.

Joy and sorrow
change places
in the heart.

Youth grows older
from the start

and, turning, spins
itself apart.

As the ash…
so the spark.

Near And Dear

To deny that, in time,
all things disappear

is to blindly dismiss
impermanence

at the expense
of the near and dear

which not embraced
in the light of day

might not be seen
as it slips away.

Hesitation

Life is precious,
and can be stolen

or, all too often,
misplaced or lost

before we even
know its value

or understand
hesitation's cost.

Flown

Time grinds its teeth
on dream and bone

winding its spring
on spinning ground

as it steps around
surrounding stars

on our dance floor
of water and stone

and sighs, "Oh my,
where have I flown?"

Crumble
Mumble

Laugh or cry
at how and why

days—once years—
keep sliding by

between the laughter
and salty tears

that erode smiles
as time slips gears

crumbling to mumbles
as silence nears.

Or

Or—it's a day
of many aspects.

Constants and changes.

Choices and chances.

Checks and challenges.

Glares and glances.

Prods and plunges.

Stumbles and stances.

And pleasant prospects
we might not expect.

Bits And Pieces

Plans, perspectives
and prospects change.

Sometimes options
seem to vanish

and we look for ways
we might accomplish

whatever we can—
if not what we wish—

with bits and pieces
we might rearrange.

Simplicity

Steering through
cloudy to clarity

we find our way
past fantasy

by the light
of calm reflection

to a deeper
appreciation

for the wisdom
of simplicity

and the fallacy
of perfection.

Anyway

Accept the night
that holds us in
its turn towards
brighter hours.

Enjoy daylight
that warms us,
with brilliance
so briefly ours

despite, knowing
we wear away
between their
grinding powers.

Melding

Rains have their falling.
Dawns have their gleams.

Toddlers their crawling.
Dreamers their dreams.

Truckers their hauling.
Players their teams.

Shoppers their malling.
Stitchers their seams.

Suburbs their sprawling.
Builders their beams.

Writers their scrawling.
Composers their themes.

Idlers their stalling.
Scoundrels their schemes.

Bullies their brawling.
Sides their extremes.

Rivers the melding
of many streams.

People

Steeple-people;
pagan-people.

Proud, loud
and cowed people.

Strong or fragile,
old or agile.

Steady, unstable.
Cruel or cordial.

All tilt the balance
we each enable.

Short

Life's too short
to linger long
over the prospects
of things we dread.

Tomorrow's too soon
to ignore today,
dwelling on what
might lie ahead.

And love's too sweet
to not be sung,
let alone, left unsaid.

Hands Held

Fingers folded
through themselves
weave a wish
for better days.

Hands pressed flat,
palm to palm
point a bow
of humble praise.

And hands held
between two hearts
share their strength
in tender ways.

Leap

Love is a leap
of kind and degree.

From first attraction
to deep affection.

Part chemistry,
part empathy.

Too often confused
with the fantasy

of a wishful
imagination.

And, even shared,
will not be spared

the laws of loss
and separation.

But worth the risk
of intimacy

considering life's
uncertainty.

Magnetic

When opposites attract
in equal portions

of powerful passions
with the common goal

of two halves that
might make a whole

there is potential
for strong connection—

a melding force
beyond their control—

if approached from
the right direction.

Familiar

The sunset we see
may not be the same.

Or the day of our week
have a similar name.

But the beat of hearts
that may never meet

still sound as if
they each repeat

a shared impulse
both have known

that only seems
like theirs alone.

Though, as sure as
the Sun will rise and set

the feelings we have,
have already met.

Drum

Time beats a clock
to a tick.

Traffic beats blacktop
to a hum.

Life can beat your back
like a stick.

But love beats the heart
like a drum.

Lovers

Though love may lead
to loss and sorrow

lovers still need to
trust tomorrow.

If Spring would heed
what Winters know

fear would feed
on cold shadow

and nothing might seed,
or anything grow.

Context

Painful losses,
present or past

lose their sting,
or often last

at least as long
as it might take

to learn to live
with the ache.

But considering
the end that
could come next

should put it
all in context.

Common

As personal as painful
experiences feel

and as deep a loss
as the days they steal—

the pleasures we know,
or merely seek

may be as real,
as they seem unique.

But, rather than rare,
are common as dust

which doesn't diminish
their effect on us

but it helps to know
they're ubiquitous.

Boredom

If life is all
we'll ever know

shouldn't boredom
be a mortal's sin?

And even if there
was more than this

why waste a day
on a dream of bliss

or expect more than
the moment we're in

when fate might spin
on the point of a pin?

Ask

We were who we were,
close to the soil

tied to tribe
and daily toil.

We knew who we were
and where we could go

but wondered what more
there was to know.

We knew what we knew,
and made up the rest

until we put what
we guessed to the test

and ventured into
the ever new

to ask and explore
what might be true.

Fine-Tuning

Poet or scientist
test the tune of a thought.

Playwright or novelist
write a right thing to say.

Musician or artist
time the tone they play.

And seeker or sage
weigh what they're taught

as sunrise or sunset
create the same day.

Measure

Star-scribes trace
nocturnal designs

in search of
celestial signs.

Peddlers of prophecy
predict what will be

and followers of fate
will await destiny.

But historians
reveal connections

as scientists
measure reactions

with precision
and curiosity

for a clearer view
of reality.

Appearance

People are so much
more than they seem.

More than they say
or rumors we hear.

More than the heroes
or villains they dream.

More than the ideal,
or the evil we fear.

Contrast

Some have wise stars
and bright angels.

Some see omens
where others see chance.

Some speak truth
while others deceive.

But we all enhance
the words we weave.

So why should it matter
what another believes

compared to what
the heart perceives?

Visions

Versions of visions
some said they saw—

but I don't expect
to ever see—

surface throughout
human history

with fantasies
of mysteries

that bend the laws
of nature—

alter our view
of reality—

and rewrite the
rules of culture.

Blind Spots

Excluding excuses
for cruelty

some faults I see
in an enemy

might also be aspects
of my own reflection—

blind spots in a
blurred perception.

But, even with reason
to be angry

I still own my
own reactions.

Them

We make
good points.

They might
make theirs.

We hide our pride.
They put on airs.

We have our faults—
they must have more.

But it might all depend
on who's keeping score.

Dispute

Though we might
not always agree

we do share much
that has held true

throughout the span
of our history.

We may have good
reason to argue

but pain is still pain
and wrong to impose.

And as blame can
inflame fragile egos

revenge has a way
of worsening woes.

Misled

Leaders who refuse
to compromise

abuse the powers
they exercise

through actions that
favor a small percent

of those they're
meant to represent.

Pretense

Since we could speak
we've told stories.

And the tales of heroes
are powerful tools

too often told
by dishonest fools

who want to write
their own rules

by repeating a lie
over and over

until they think
you think it's true.

They pretend to share
whatever you value

but then just do
what they want to do.

Politicos

As primeval cats
taught birds to fly—

by chasing them
into the sky—

predator-politicos
force friends and foes

to open their eyes
and rise above lies

or fall prey to
painful surprise.

Primal

Two eyes, two ears,
two hands, two feet.

A clever creature,
not quite complete

due to a primal
urge to compete

driven by a sense
of crude conceit.

But still evolving
by stumble and stride

to overcome
a primitive pride

that can turn rivalry
into homicide.

Reprisal

The hate speech
of blind rage

can push one
side to strike first

and the other to
settle the score.

But one reprisal
only leads to more.

And, at its worst,
the madness of war.

Choice

To not be told
what to believe

or not to trust
what we perceive.

And not be forced
to conform

to the norms
of stern society

or the dictates of
rigid authority

is necessary
to being free.

Repair

One bad minute
might ruin an hour.

One wrong choice
might spoil a season.

And even sweet love
can turn sour.

But every change
has its reason

and reason often
has the power

to find a way
to start over.

Similarity

I've known the
edges of your pain

and the laughter
of your joy.

I've felt your
urges to create

and sometimes
to destroy.

I've seen your love,
heard your hate

and known enough
of you to see

some of the same
deep traits in me.

Sown

How many seeds—
burst from a pod—

find the right soil
when they're dispersed?

I'd like to believe
that our better deeds

will find firmer ground
than our worst.

Ripples

Thoughts and feelings
that interface

by shared reflection
or warm embrace

expand our spheres
of connection

on wider ripples
that interlace

and blend into
our human race.

Novelty

We want
what we want
until it's ours.

Then we begin to
count the hours

that time and
repetition sour

when the novelty
loses its novel power.

Comforts

We count on our
creature-comforts—

blankets, pillows
and sweet desserts—

while the barely warm
and sparingly fed

curl up against
the damp and cold

without the pleasure
of a real bed

or the certainty
of daily bread.

Night after night,
young and old

unable to see
their way ahead.

While we face a loss
of flavor with dread.

Secondhand Store

A two-room museum
of lost memories.
Bookshelves of clues
to dusty mysteries.

Racked fabrics
of faded styles.
Repurposed fashions
and closet exiles.

Silent survivors
of death and divorce.
Tired toys that
ran their course.

The odd knickknacks
and curios.
Postcards and photos
meant as mementos.

The shadows of attics
where secrets slept,
now laid out on tables
where nothing is kept.

Dare

Time might turn
fair moments rare

and bring on days
hard to bear.

But the cares
we dare to share

soften our stress
and defy despair.

The cares we share
defy despair.

Wings

It's the clarity
of simple things:

the honesty
of innocence

the tangible truth
of common sense

and the lighter side
of strong feelings

or what we trust,
that gives us wings.

Acknowledgements

With gratitude to *The Lyric* and *The Seventh Quarry*, in which the following poems first appeared:

The Lyric: Pelicans; Curlews; Wing Span; Air Traffic

The Seventh Quarry: Clock; Solo; Curse; Feeder; The Boathouse; Flown; Or; Fine-Tuning

www.ingramcontent.com/pod-product-compliance
Lightning Source LLC
Chambersburg PA
CBHW060401080526
44583CB00012B/413